MOTHER TO SONS

Love Letters to My Sons

by

Dr. Mary L. Wise

Mother to Sons

ISBN: 978-0-578-77906-5

Credits
Editorial: Carla DuPont
Cover Design: HER Peace, LLC Publishing
Published By: HER Peace, LLC Publishing
Orlando, FL 32818
321.310.1113
www.sandarawilliams.com

DEDICATION

This book is dedicated to all who have been victimized and senselessly killed.
#blacklivesmatter #saytheirnames
#icantbreathe

SEAN BELL
BREONNA TAYLOR
ERIC GARNER
TRAYVON MARTIN
YUSEF HAWKINS

ACKNOWLEDGMENTS

I would like to acknowledge all of the mothers and mother figures who have sons who they will share this journey with. To my heavenly Father for providing me with the vision and the words to share with my sons, your sons, and our sons. I am grateful for my Author Coach Sandara Williams for the six week intensive writing course and for the accountability of all of my peer authors in the course.

I also acknowledge the unconditional love of my husband, Antonio Wise, Sr., who supports me in all my endeavors. To my heartbeats, Antonio Wise, Jr., Austin Wise, Alexander Wise, and Zayden Granada-Wise, my sons and grandson who gave me the inspiration for this book. I also stand on the shoulders of my extended family and friends in Florida, Texas, Georgia, New York, Missouri, and D.C.

Thank you all for being in my life and a part of my journey.

CONTENTS

When a mother prays for her wayward son,
No words can make clear the vivid reality of her supplications,
She does not really think that she is persuading God
To be good to her son,
For the courage of her prayer is due to her certain faith
That God also must wish that boy to be recovered from his sin.
She rather is taking on her heart the same burden that God has on his;
Is joining her demand with the divine desire.
In this system of personal life which makes up the moral universe,
She is taking her place alongside God
In an urgent, creative outpouring of sacrificial love.
Her intercession is the utterance of her life;
It is love on its knees.

~HARRY EMERSON FOSDICK~

FOREWORD

There is no greater feeling than to be a mother. When I use the term ‘mother’, I’m describing any woman who has been provided the awesome responsibility of parenting. Whether you are a mother, sister, grandmother, auntie, adoptive mother, or any other woman who is raising or has raised sons, this is for you.

Like most mothers, we have a lot of things to tell our sons but not always a lot of time to get it out. I decided to write letters to my sons that cover a wide range of topics for them to use in any situation. I just want to ensure that my sons, your sons, and all of our sons have resources to guide them along the way.

I am in no way attempting to downplay the very important role that a father has in the upbringing of their son. However, I want to emphasize that the role of a mother is also pivotal. As a mother, we truly understand and know everything about our sons, we are the nurturers, we become our sons' friends, we are their first cheerleaders, first teachers, and we become their fiercest protectors. Whether you birthed a son, you've adopted a son, you're a grand-mother, you're an aunt, you're a sister, if you have a role in the upbringing of a son, that role is very important.

To my sons,

I write these letters from my heart and from the very depths of my soul so that if I am not around, if you lose your way, you will always be anchored. I thank God for this awesome opportunity to be your mom. The letters in this book are in no particular order so you can read one chapter that appeals to you one day and another chapter another day or you can read them in sequential order. It doesn't matter which order you read them, just read.

Love you to infinity and beyond,
Mom

MOTHER TO SONS

Love Letters to My Sons

1

Letter One

Facts

"In fact, everything is yours, including the world, life, death, the present and the future. Everything belongs to you, and you belong to Christ, and Christ belongs to God."

1 Corinthians 3:22-23 CEV

To my talented young kings,

You are probably asking yourself, why is my mother deciding to write me now? Here are the facts, and the reason why I decided that right now is the most appropriate time! This is the appointed time and the only time that I am promised to be here.

On May 25, 2020, I, like most of the world, watched in horror as four Minnesota police officers placed their knees on the neck of George Floyd for 8 minutes and 46 seconds! I watched as he shouted, "I can't breathe!" My heart broke when he called for his mama, who had already passed away. I had to turn it off because I found myself asking, what will it take for society to see my sons, their friends, and all young African American men as people? What will it take for them to recognize that you are descendants of The Most High? A royal priesthood?

We are adamant for society to understand the reasons that 'Black Lives Matter' because there are hundreds of young men and women who have been brutally killed, victimized, or abused by those who have vowed to protect and serve simply due to the color of their skin. I am outraged by that.

Even more so , I am determined to give you facts, while the world spews hateful lies. I will speak life, while the world attempts to kill you both literally and figuratively.

Psalms 139:13 - 16 (MSG) "Oh yes, you shaped me first inside, then out; you formed me in my mother's womb. I thank you, High God - you're breathtaking! Body and soul I am marvelously made! I worship in adoration - what a creation! You know me inside and out you know every bone in my body you know exactly how I was made, bit by bit, how I was sculpted from nothing into something. Like an open book you watch me grow from conception to birth; all the stages of my life were spread out before you, the days of my life all prepared before I even lived one day."

No matter what you find yourself faced with, know that the God who is above all things, knows all things, and created all things loves you immensely. This is a foundational truth that so many of us forget. John 15: 18-19 (AMP), "If the world hates you{and it does}, know that it hated ME before it hated you. If you belonged to the world, the world would love {you as} its own and would treat you with affection. But you are not of the world {you no longer belong to it}, but I have chosen you out of the world. And because of this the world hates you."

Just let that sink in for a moment. For over 400 years, the world has tried to dictate our narrative. While we are nowhere near God's promises for us, the world can never permanently defeat us. You are young, talented, gifted, and black; nothing and no one can change that narrative.

Take the righteous anger that you are feeling right now with the death of George Floyd, Ahmaud Arbery, Breonna Taylor, and countless others and find ways to effect change. Participate in peaceful protests, but be safe. Know your routes to get back to your car before curfew and leave if you sense things are escalating. "But after the protesting, what else should I be doing?" I'm glad you asked, because you know I was going to tell you anyway! Here is a list of some things you should do to keep the momentum going. The list is in no particular order:

1. Register to vote. Not only register, but vote in ALL elections held for your area.

2. Support black owned business. Better yet, start your own business!

3. Volunteer your time to mentor and support other African American young men. My recommend-dations would be to start with Boys and Girls Club, Big Brother, or even through our church.

4. Get involved in a local civil rights organization. Find one that fits you and not just because I said so (NAACP, Urban League, BLM, etc.).

5. Volunteer to serve on community boards.

6. Arm yourself with knowledge of economics. Knowledge is king. The more you know, the less you have to depend on the system.

7. Read…ok, let me be real here, listen to news, not just on the 'Gram or on Twitter, but find Black talk radio and news shows about us and for us.

8. Become financially literate. I have a letter about this, too!

What we are facing is systemic racism in every aspect of society. In the *Miseducation of the Negro* by Dr. Carter G. Woodson (P.S. this book is in our family library) written in 1933, Dr. Carter asserted that our miseducation has come about due to the teaching structure that does not provide a foundational teaching of our Black culture and heritage. We only get Black History Month which is not consistently taught in our public school system. When you think about it, Black history is an afterthought and woefully absent in mainstream educational systems. I need for you to understand the importance of black history and culture, and educate yourself.

Sir Winston Churchill stated, "Those who fail to learn from history are doomed to repeat it." For over 400 years, we have been fighting the same fight but not learning from history. It's time for all of us to wake up!

I'll end this letter by quoting James Baldwin. Although this was quoted in 1963, think about how relevant this is to what we are currently facing with Black Lives Matter.

> "It is not really a "Negro revolution" that is upsetting the country. What is upsetting the country is a sense of its own identity. If, for example, one managed to change the curriculum in all the schools so that Negroes learned more about themselves and their real contributions to this culture, you would be liberating not only Negroes, you'd be liberating white people who know nothing about their own history. And the reason is that if you are compelled to lie about one aspect of anybody's history, you must lie about it all. If you have to lie about my real role here, if you have to pretend that I hoed all that cotton just because I loved you, then you have done something to yourself. You are mad."

Get involved in your local school board, go volunteer at your former high school, become a Big Brother, educate yourself and your friends on our history, that's how you change the narrative.

Love you to infinity and beyond,
Mom

Letter One Discussion

What were the key takeaways you got from this letter?

____

____

____

____

____

____

____

What facts do you believe about yourself?

____

____

____

____

____

____

____

What steps do you need to take in order for you to see yourself as God sees you?

____

____

____

____

____

____

____

What are your thoughts about the senseless violence against Black lives?

____

____

____

____

____

____

____

What things are you going to personally do to effect change in your community?

____

____

____

____

____

____

____

Letter Two

Faith

2

"Faith makes us sure of what we hope for and gives us proof of what we cannot see. It was their faith that made our ancestors pleasing to God."

Hebrews 11: 1-2, CEV

To my talented young kings,

I bet you're saying to yourself that you are going to skip over this chapter because Mom is going to get all preachy on you. I'm not, but I am going to share with you some things that I hope will build up your faith muscles. I'm not going to demand that you go to church, but what I do want to stress in this letter is the importance of having a personal relationship with God. And I want to do that with scriptures and personal examples, okay?

I'm a mom who prays; no secret, no shame. I pray not only for you but for sons all over this world. In Ephesians 3:14-19 (MSG), it says, "My response is to get down on my knees before the Father, this magnificent Father who parcels out all heaven and earth. I ask him to strengthen you by his Spirit - not a brute strength but a glorious inner strength - that Christ will live in you as you open the door and invite him in. And I ask him that with both feet planted firmly on love, you'll be able to take in with all followers of Jesus the extravagant dimensions of Christ's love. Reach out and experience the breadth! Test its length! Plumb the depths! Rise to the heights! Live full lives, full in the fullness of God."

I want you to live a full life and you get that by having a relationship with our Heavenly Father. I'm not going to guilt you or condemn you about not going to church, there is enough of that going on already. If nothing else, COVID-19 has shown us that church is more than a structural building; church must be in your hearts. Find a church you relate to that relates to you. I don't care if it's online or a physical church, whatever helps you further develop your relationship with God.

Where do you start? I'm glad you asked. You can start by adding a bible app on your phone. Spend the first 15 minutes of your day reading scriptures and praying. It's that simple. If you don't remember how to pray or what to pray for, just pray the Lord's Prayer. "Our Father which art in heaven, Hallowed be thy name. Thy kingdom come. Thy will be done in earth, as it is in heaven. Give us this day our daily bread. And forgive us our debts, as we forgive our debtors. And lead us not into temptation, but deliver us from evil: For thine is the kingdom, and the power, and the glory, for ever. Amen" (Matthew 6:9-15 KJV).

Why focus on faith? Because without faith, it is impossible to please God. Faith is God's gift to you. Ephesians 2:8 (CEV) reads, "You were saved by faith in God, who treats us much better than we deserve. This is God's gift to you, and not anything you have done on your own."

Let's make it personal, what does faith have to do with anything? Let me show you. When you practiced hours and hours on the football field, having two-a-days during the summer, playing scrimmages, then football season finally began and you believed your team was going to win with your help, right? That right there is faith! You had faith in what your coaches were teaching you. You had faith that your teammates were going to play their positions. And you had faith that you were going to be able to demonstrate your talents!

That's exactly what God wants you to do with Him. Rely on Him, trust in Him, love Him, and believe in Him. When things are going in your favor, have faith in Him. When things aren't going in your favor, have faith in Him. When you're facing new challenges or obstacles, have faith in Him. When you don't know who to trust or what to believe, have faith in Him. When you lose your way, have faith in Him. When your days are dark, have faith in Him.

As your mom, I know it may appear that I have all the answers (most of the time, this is true) and I appear to have it all together. Please know that, like you, I had to find my own way and my own relationship with God. I'm thankful for those who prayed for me. It wasn't until I found my own faith relationship that things turned around for me. Don't be fooled by those people who swear they've never done anything wrong or they have been holy ALL their lives. We all have sinned and come short of the will of God. But praise God that we awake every morning with brand new mercies.

I know you are saying to yourself, if God is truly present always, why don't I feel His presence? Why is it that at times I feel lonely, dissatisfied, tired, anxious, and afraid? God's presence starts with having faith in what Scripture says. In order for you to feel God's presence, it starts with you trusting that God is right next to you and wants you to know Him. God doesn't force Himself on you. Make space for God in your heart today, trust in His word that "He will not leave you or forsake you," and encounter the nearness of your Heavenly Father. Your only job is to make space in your heart and trust God to take care of the rest. He will take care of the rest.

I'll leave you with this, "God can do anything, you know - far more than you could ever imagine or guess or request in your wildest dreams! He does it not by pushing us around but by working within us, his Sprite deeply and gently within us" (Ephesians 3:20, MSG).

Love you to infinity and beyond,
Mom

Letter Two Discussion

What were the key takeaways that you got from this letter?

____

____

____

____

____

____

____

What are your thoughts about having faith?

____

____

____

____

____

____

____

What steps can you take to increase your faith?

What things have happened in your life to believe in faith? Or not believe in faith?

Why is it important to have faith?

____

____

____

____

____

____

____

Letter Three

Family

"But if you don't want to worship the Lord, then choose right now!... My family and I are going to worship and obey the Lord."

Joshua 24:15, CEV

To my talented young kings,

This topic is near and dear to my heart. Coming from a rather large family, our get togethers were huge. On my mom's side, she was one of 13 and on my dad's side, it was only he and his sister. However, on each side we had large extended families. Growing up was spent with cousins during summer breaks, birthdays and most major holidays. I have so many memories of those times, some good and others not so good. There were family members who were closer than others; but, at the end of the day we were family.

Desmond Tutu stated, "You don't choose your family. They are God's gift to you, as you are to them." So let's start by talking about our immediate family, you are a gift to this family. Let me repeat, you are a gift to this family. While we may not agree on everything, as a part of the family we owe it to each other to hear each other out. The reason we have family meetings is because your voice is important and I wanted you to know that early on. While your dad and I had the final say, we believed that including you on important decisions impacting our family was important.

In Ephesians 6:4, it simply states, "Parents, don't be hard on your children. Raise them properly. Teach them and instruct them about the Lord" (CEV). God entrusted us with the gift of being your family. Our job as parents is to teach you, guide you, and show you the way. I know sometimes it feels like we are dictating, while we are strongly encouraging. Our hope is that when you are older, you will not forget our teachings.
Now, let me say this, there are some family members who you won't be close to and that's okay. Remember that just because they are your kin, they may not be your type. Some family members keep up unnecessary drama; those are the ones who you love from a distance. Some family members don't want to see you succeed and they always bring up what you did wrong; you also just love them from a distance. Family should be there to build you up, not tear you down.

Some friends will be there for you more than your family. Keep those friends in your immediate circle. They are few and far between (we will talk about them in our Friends Letter).

As you get older, I know that you want to do your own things, hang out with your own friends and not spend as much time with us. While I understand that, when you have an immediate family structure that's close, you want to make sure not to lose out on precious family time. You and your siblings should always have each other's backs, unless it's something immoral or unlawful.

The reason I'm stressing family is because I have so many memories to look back on that I wouldn't have if I didn't make time. Let me share with you a few of the fondest memories.

Family Memory #1: My mother's side of the family was so large, we got together every Thanksgiving. With just us, we easily had 50+ people in attendance. After dinner, we always had a fashion/talent show!

Family Memory #2: Before Tyler Perry became famous with Madea, one of my mom's sister's was actually Madea in the flesh. After college, I stayed with one of my aunts, she saw someone peeking in her bedroom one night and called her sister. Within 5 minutes, our real life Madea was there letting off shots in the backyard, then drove back home! We found the peeping Tom and let's just say some of my cousins took care of the problem.

Family Memory #3: I remember spending summers on my grandfather's farm in Oviedo, FL. Those were some of the most carefree times in my life, riding horses, making wine, picking corn, okra, and funning around with cousins.

Family Memory #4: After my mom died, when we were still living in Florida, I made it a point to go visit most Saturday mornings for food, gossip and laughter.

Family Memory #5: Our family vacation to New Orleans the first time having all adult kids walking up and down Bourbon Street, enjoying daiquiris, hurricanes, and great Cajun food.

I could go on and on, but make time for your parents and elderly relatives as you get older. I know you will soon have families of your own; still, make sure your significant other understands that we take vacations together. Keep in contact with your siblings and cousins. Also, please don't forget to call your Meme once a week :) You never know when you won't be able to do it anymore.

I'll end like I started, with a scripture. Exodus 20:12 says in part, "Respect your father and your mother, and you will live a long time in the land I am giving you" (CEV). Text me, DM, and call me!

Love you to infinity and beyond,
Mom

Letter Three Discussion

What were the key takeaways that you got from this letter?

____

____

____

____

____

____

____

Do you believe that family is important? Why? Or why not?

____

____

____

____

____

____

____

Are there some family members that you need to make peace with?

____

Do you have any great family memories? Do you have them written down?

What steps do you need to take to make your family your priority?

____

____

____

____

____

____

____

Please note, if you have family members that have verbally, physically and/or emotionally abused you, please share with a trusted person and get the support you need.

Letter Four
Finding Purpose

4

"For everything, absolutely everything, above and below, visible and invisible, rank after rank of angels- everything got started in him and finds its purpose in him."

Colossians 1:16 (MSG)

To my talented young kings,

I had a mentor who used to ask this question, "What is your purpose?" At first, I didn't get why she would always ask that. Eventually, I learned that without purpose you waste a lot of time and energy trying to be all things to all people. Don't waste any more time! Ephesians 1:11-12 says, "It's in Christ that we find out who we are and what we are living for. Long before we first heard of Christ and got our hopes up, He had His eye on us, had designs on us for glorious living, part of the overall purpose He is working out in everything and everyone."

In 2002, Pastor Rick Warren published, *The Purpose Driven Life* (also in our family library). I will tell you this book helped me tremendously by putting some things in perspective. You probably don't remember, but I also bought each of you the youth version of this book. Why is finding your purpose so important, because you will waste years trying to be happy and trying to do everything people want you to do. God created you and knew about you before I even thought about conceiving you. In this New York Times Best Seller, Pastor Warren says we all have five purposes to fulfill on this earth, they are:

1. You were planned for God's pleasure
2. You were formed for God's family
3. You were Created to become like Christ
4. You were shaped for serving God
5. You were made for a mission

I'm not promising that problems will automatically go away, but knowing your purpose equips you with the tools you will need when setbacks occur (P.S. - go back to the Faith Letter and re-read).

You must first recognize the gifts that God has given you to use for your defined purpose. These gifts include things that you can't control, like your parents, your race, your ethnicity, your height, eye color, native language, or where you were born. But they also include those spiritual gifts, your loving heart, your unique abilities, your unique, personality, and your unique life experiences.

What does all this really mean in simple terms? God created you for Himself, he wanted you to be right here, right now because He loves you so much. He created you to praise Him and acknowledge Him in everything you do. He wants you to connect to a church family and share your gifts. He wants you to live your life, like He lived his: loving others more than himself and doing everything to please God.

You have special gifts, skills, and abilities that only you have! No one can do the exact thing that you do so very well. God provided each of us our gifts to be used not just for your personal pleasure but God's pleasure! "There are different kinds of spiritual gifts, but they all come from the same Spirit. There are different ways to serve the same Lord, and we can each do different things. Yet the same God works in all of us and helps us in everything we do. The Spirit has given each of us a special way of serving others" (1 Corinthians 12:4-7, CEV). You have a special mission in this earth to perform. You are the only one who has the gifts, skills, and abilities to do it. Don't sit on them!

One of my favorite quotes is by Audrey Lourde which said, "If I didn't define myself for myself, I would be crunched into other people's fantasies for me and eaten alive." Don't let someone else dictate who you are, what you should be, or what you should be doing with your life. Finding and living out your purpose frees you to be exactly who God called you to be.

The late Nipsey Hussle had the same message, "Define who you are and what you are, and be clear on that. Meditate on that and then, live and die by that... You can't break the rules, the fundamental rules. Be a man of your word; do what you say you're gonna do, respect people the way you would like to be respected."

In Matthew 11:28 it reads, "Come to Me, all you who labor and are heavy laden, and I will give you rest (NKJV)." This is referring to those who are laboring to be perfect and beating themselves down with guilty feelings when they fail. "Therefore there is now no condemnation [no guilty verdict, no punishment] for those who are in Christ Jesus [who believe in Him as personal Lord and Savior]" (Romans 8:1, KJV).

Lastly in Romans 8:31-33, "What can we say about all this? If God is on our side, can anyone be against us? God did not keep back his own Son, but he gave him for us. If God did this, won't he freely give us everything else? (CEV)" Don't worry about what people say about you, you just worry about what God says and be who He called you to be.

Love you to infinity and beyond,
Mom

Letter Four Discussion

What were the key takeaways that you got from this letter?

____

____

____

____

____

____

____

Do you know your purpose?

____

____

____

____

____

____

____

What special gifts, skills and abilities do you have?

____

____

____

____

____

____

____

Do you believe that you were created to bring delight to God?

____

____

____

____

____

____

____

If you aren't sure about your purpose, what steps are you going to take to discover your purpose?

____
____
____
____
____
____
____

If you know your purpose, are you living a purpose-filled life? Why? Or why not?

____
____
____
____
____
____
____

Letter Five

5

Finances

"A good man leaveth an inheritance to his children's children.."

Proverbs 13:22, KJV

To my talented young kings,

Did you know that there are over 800 scriptures dedicated to money, finances, wealth, and debt in the bible? I didn't either until recently. Did you know that God wants us to be rich? I want to share with you God's thoughts on money, finance, debt, and wealth. I will also add some practical tips and recommendations to accompany these thoughts.

Generational Wealth

In Deuteronomy 28:1-13, (NLT), God sets the foundation for us to have generational wealth. He simply says,

1If you fully obey the Lord your God and
carefully follow all his commands I give you
today, the Lord your God will set you high above
all the nations on earth. 2All these blessings will
come on you and accompany you if you obey the
Lord your God:
3You will be blessed in the city and blessed in
the country.
4The fruit of your womb will be blessed, and
the crops of your land and the young of your
livestock—the calves of your herds and the lambs
of your flocks.

5Your basket and your kneading trough will be blessed.

6You will be blessed when you come in and blessed when you go out.

7The Lord will grant that the enemies who rise up against you will be defeated before you. They will come at you from one direction but flee from you in seven.

8The Lord will send a blessing on your barns and on everything you put your hand to. The Lord your God will bless you in the land he is giving you.

9The Lord will establish you as his holy people, as he promised you on oath, if you keep the commands of the Lord your God and walk in obedience to him.

10Then all the peoples on earth will see that you are called by the name of the Lord, and they will fear you.

11The Lord will grant you abundant prosperity—in the fruit of your womb, the young of your livestock and the crops of your ground—in the land he swore to your ancestors to give you.

12The Lord will open the heavens, the storehouse of his bounty, to send rain on your land in season and to bless all the work of your hands. You will lend to many nations but will borrow from none.

13The Lord will make you the head, not the tail. If you pay attention to the commands of the Lord your God that I give you this day and carefully follow them, you will always be at the top, never at the bottom."

So how do you build generational wealth? You first have to follow God's commandments, then make sure that you are spending, saving, and investing your money, time, and talents wisely. How do you do that?

Savings

"On the first day of the week each one of you is to put something aside, in proportion to his prosperity, and she it so that no collections [will need to] be made when I come (1 Corinthians 16:2 (AMP)." This scripture is simply saying that you need to save, if you get paid weekly, bi-weekly, or even monthly. Put aside 10% in a savings account and put aside 10% for tithing. You should be able to live off of 80% of your net income, if not you need to scale back. If you are 18 years or older, you should have your own checking and savings account. The 10% should be moved from your checking to your savings whenever you get paid. Do not touch it unless it's an emergency such as paying medical bills or a life and death situation, not going out to the club or on trip with your friends! If you are not old enough, your parents will have to set you up an account. There are a lot of options on finding a bank that is right for your personal needs.

Since you are under 30, recommendations state that you should be saving 20% of your paycheck, spending 50% of your paycheck on essential expenses (food, rent, utilities), and only 30% for discretionary spending (car, gas, dates, clubs). Work up to where you are comfortable, understanding that saving now leads to financial freedom later down the line.

Mom Tip:
Do a Google search to find the bank that offers you more pros than cons.

Proverbs 22:7 (NLT) states, "Just as the rich rule the poor, so the borrower is servant to the lender." When you owe someone money, they rule over you. You become slave to their demands. I'm not saying that you can't borrow money, I'm just saying be prudent on what you are borrowing money for. Research says 8 out of 10 Americans are in debt, that's not including mortgages. That means most Americans use credit cards to fund their lifestyles such as clothes, cars, entertainment, and gas. Consider what I said earlier about saving. If you allocated a portion of your paycheck to essentials, and do not go over that, you won't find yourself in debt. What happens when you find yourself in debt? You work a dead end job so you can pay for the debt. You never fulfill your dreams because you are stuck paying on debt that will take you 30 years to dig yourself out of! Not having debt is so liberating, instead of staying on a job that you just tolerate, you will be more free to explore your options!

Credit

I do want to spend a little time making sure you build up your credit. Take advantage of pulling your annual free credit report. Knowing your credit scores and having good credit scores will mean the difference in what interest rates you may be eligible for when purchasing a car or a mortgage. Use credit to increase your buying power not be enslaved by it. If you find something that is not yours, dispute it so that it won't mess up your score.

Mom Tip:
Go to freecreditreport.com annually to pull and review your credit score.

Investments

This is where you really build generational wealth. Invest in real estate including houses, duplexes, multi-family units and make money while you are sleeping. Invest in the stock market. Start small and study others who have been successful in the market. Look at purchasing municipal bonds. Look at franchises, invest in various businesses, and grow your own business. All of these items will help to set you up financially while also allowing you the financial freedom to set up a family business structure for you, your kids, and grandkids to have generational wealth.

There is a lot more to share but this should you push you in the right direction. Don't get into the wrong type of debt, save your money, and build your credit with the ultimate goal of creating and building generational wealth. I will end with this scripture, I Timothy 6:10, "…Lust for money brings trouble and nothing but trouble. Going down that path, some lose their footing in the faith completely and live to regret it bitterly ever after" (MSG).

Love you to infinity and beyond,
Mom

Letter Five Discussion

What were the key takeaways that you got from this letter?

____

____

____

____

____

____

____

Do you know your credit score? How to pull your credit report?

____

____

____

____

____

____

____

Do you have a checking and/or savings account?

Are you applying the 70/20/10 principles to savings?

What is the difference between good debt and bad debt?

____

____

____

____

____

____

____

What steps do you need to take to become the lender not the borrower?

____

____

____

____

____

____

____

Have you thought about what business(es) you would like to own?

____

____

____

____

____

____

____

Letter Six
Filthiness

"Then Jacob said unto his household, and to all that were with him, Put away the strange gods that are among you, and be clean, and change your garments:"

Genesis 35:2 AMP

To my talented young kings,

Okay, so you know I had to add a letter about filthiness and cleanness in here! You know I'm border line OCD (obsessive compulsive disorder) but having boys forced me to let go of some of my compulsive cleaning habits and just focus on what I believe the basic necessities were.

Once you are on your own, I hope you take these principles with you. I can only pray and hope you will. We are going to cover some of the basics just in case you forgot them already :)

Bathroom

I'm starting with the bathroom because that is one room in the house that you should always want to stay clean. But you also know why I won't share a bathroom with you unless we are on vacation! Newsflash! Your aim hasn't gotten better as you've gotten older, so always turn on the light and watch your aim. Clean your toilet out weekly. Wipe the seats and top with bleach. Keep two extra rolls of toilet tissue in your bathroom so you won't get caught with your pants down, literally! Clean your sink daily; put hair in trash, not down the drain. Clean your shower weekly. Have at least four sets of towels that are for your use only and have different sets for your guests. Change out your towel at least every other day. I know you are rolling your eyes, but you know this is one of my pet peeves.

Bedroom

Make your bed up when you get out of it. It feels better to come home from work to a freshly made bed. Another one of my mom rules. Buy at least two sheet sets so you can alternate washing your bed linen at least twice monthly. Clean your room; no woman worth anything wants to be in the dirty, smelly bedroom of the man they are with.

Kitchen

If you use it, then wash it, clean it, and put it up. Don't leave it for someone else to clean up. Wipe your counters down nightly. Empty your trash cans frequently; certain foods smell if left overnight so make sure that you empty them even if the trash isn't full to keep your house or apartment from smelling like trash.

Washing

As you all were growing up and participating in sports, I noticed that sometimes your clothes and towels took two times through the washer to get them clean and smelling fresh. Having older relatives is a blessing, so here are some tips for you. Separate your dark clothes from your light clothes. Use whatever detergent you believe works best for you. However, you know I used Sports Order Defense detergent and then added Pine-Sol to the machine to keep your clothes smelling fresh. For your light clothes, especially if you have under arm stains or neck stains on your collared shirts, soak them in vinegar prior to washing and put the washer on the hottest setting the clothes can take. Also, add Pine-Sol to washer.

Your Body

When you first get up, please brush your teeth. I love you, but I love you better without your hot breath assaulting my nose! Brush in morning and prior to going to bed, floss frequently and use mouthwash. Keep up with setting dental appointments every six months. Your mouth thanks you and the women you are with will thank you also.

Shower daily, use the right soap, strong deodorant, cologne, and use lotion! I know you don't really like bathing, but soaking in a bathtub at least weekly does your body good and helps you get to all of those particular places that just hopping in and out of a shower may miss. Clip your fingernails and toenails regularly. After we get past this COVID-19, go get a pedicure at least every other month.

Keep up with your dental appointments (yes, I'm repeating it again) and your medical appointments. Go get a yearly physical and as you get older make sure you are doing all the required testing. As you are sexually active, I recommend that you get tested frequently and use your own condoms.

Remember to always have extra underwear, socks, undershirts, toothpaste deodorant, soap, toilet paper, paper towels, towels, sheets, and cleaning supplies. You never know who is coming to visit and you always want to be prepared. Don't have me popping up at your place and have to pull out the white gloves to do an inspection!

Lastly, I did find a few scriptures that discuss filthiness but I will leave you with this one. Ezekiel 36:25 (KJV) says, "Then I will sprinkle clean water upon you, and ye shall be clean: from all your filthiness, and from all your idols, will I cleanse you."

Love you to infinity and beyond,
Mom

Letter Six Discussion

What were the key takeaways that you got from this letter?

____

____

____

____

____

____

____

Do you know how to make some basic food items for yourself? If not, check out Pinterest.

____

____

____

____

____

____

____

Do you believe being clean is important? Why or why not?

Did you know that objects in your house have more than 300 different types of bacteria?

What steps can you take to clean up a little bit everyday?

____

____

____

____

____

____

____

7

Letter Seven

Females

"A woman's family is held together by her wisdom, but it can be destroyed by her foolishness."

Proverbs 14:1 CEV

To my talented young kings,

This is another topic that is near and dear to my heart. I want you to find the woman who God has sent to you. However, I know that while you are waiting, you are visual creatures, so you automatically look at a pretty face, small waist, big booties, and/or big breasts, and say to yourself 'that can be my girl'. I'm not so naive that I don't understand the physical is what attracts you first. I just want you to remember what the Bible says about it. In Proverbs 31: 30-31 (CEV), David says, "Charm can be deceiving, and beauty fades away, but a woman who honors the Lord deserves to be praised. Show her respect - praise her in public for what she has done."

In this Snapchat, Instagram, and Twitter society we find ourselves in, you are inundated with pictures of beautiful video vixens and find yourself looking for that in females. STOP IT! I used the word female specifically because you shouldn't be looking for a female; but a woman. When I looked for a definition of the word 'female,' what I found simply refers to the sex that can have babies, both humans and animals. However, when I look up definitions for a woman, I find the definition not only says an adult female person, but goes on to add, a woman belonging to a particular category as by birth, residence, membership, or occupation; womankind; distinctly feminine nature; wife or girlfriend.

I start right there because as your mom, I don't think any young lady is good enough; but as a woman, I want you to know what you should be looking for in a future helpmate. I'm going to be extremely blunt, so skip over this part if you're not ready to receive what I'm going to say.

First, if she puts out on first date, has dated members of your crew, or has a loose reputation, steer clear of her. You know and have friends who have foolishly participated in running trains on willing young women who then turn around and point to just one who raped or violated her. Please hear me out, I'm not saying that some women are not victims of sexual assault, what I am saying is…don't put yourself in a situation like this and you can avoid the fall out. Just be cautious.

Second, the young lady who wants to be friends with benefits should make your yellow flag should go up. Women are peculiar creatures. We may say one thing with our mouths and be thinking something totally different in our heads and our hearts. Some of us can handle giving our bodies away without catching feelings, but that's few and far between. Unlike men, when we participate in the sexual act, our feelings get involved. Again, if you are looking to build a solid foundation for a relationship, not sure if this is the right path. I will footnote and say, I know of people who started off like this and have been happily married for years. It just takes lots of open communication and defining of expectations.

Say you found someone you believe you want to date. Take time to find out not only her likes and dislikes, but her career aspirations, religious beliefs, political beliefs, views on children, marriage, and relationships. Don't stop there, find out about her relationship with her father. If there isn't one, who was a positive male figure she had in her life? If she was raised by a single mom, what thoughts, beliefs and feelings was she taught about men and their role in the relationship?

Let's face it, men and women think differently; we approach things differently. To overcome the gap, you have to learn to be open and honest about your feelings. If, after a while, you know that you want different things in life or you're tired of the constant bickering/arguing, instead of moving and starting to date someone else, be honest and let her know the relationship isn't working out. Holding on and letting her think y'all are still together isn't going to end very well.

Now, let's flip the script. What happens when you say you're in a relationship but you're sneaking around and seeing other people and she pulls a you on you (i.e. kind of like that foolishness with Jada, Will, and August). People get shot, feelings get hurt, and things can go really bad. Treat her like you would love for her to treat you.

I'm hopeful that you all will find the woman who becomes your queen. Once you find the right one, please consider these 11 recommendations:

> *1. Be fully committed to the relationship; don't take the relationship for granted.*
> *2. Respect your woman in both words and actions.*
> *3. Take responsibility for your actions. When you make a mistake, own up to it and apologize.*
> *4. Remain faithful to your woman.*
> *5. Be trustworthy, make sure you don't give your woman a reason not to trust you.*
> *6. Take the time to understand your woman.*
> *7. Take the time to make your woman happy.*

8. Be appreciative of the role your woman plays in your life and the value she brings to you.
9. Be a man of integrity.
10. Show your woman how much she means to you.
11. Look for ways to make your woman better.
*(*elcrema.com*)*

Lastly, Proverbs 18:22 (CEV) states, "A man's greatest treasure is his wife - she is a gift from the Lord." A king deserves a queen, so don't drop your crown to settle.

Love you to infinity and beyond,
Mom

Letter Seven Discussion

What were the key takeaways that you got from this letter?

Are you more impressed by great looks or a great mind?

Do you believe that waiting for the right woman is important?

____

____

____

____

____

____

____

How do you treat women? Would you want a man to treat your mom the same way?

____

____

____

____

____

____

____

Is the woman you with someone you believe you could marry? Why or why not?

____

____

____

____

____

____

____

Letter Eight

Fatherhood

8

"For those whom the LORD loves He corrects, Even as a father corrects the son in whom he delights."

Proverbs 3:12 AMP

To my talented young kings,

This is another topic that is near and dear to my heart. When I think about the systemic racism prevalent in our society, I think about how many of our kids are growing up in either single parent households, raised by grandparents, other family members, adoptive parents, or in foster care. We are living in times when society minimizes the impact and the need for fathers to play a pivotal role in the upbringing of their kids. Rapper Nas said, “All fatherhood is very important because single mothers shouldn’t have to raise sons or daughters; they need that help.”

That’s why the previous letter on Females is an important one. If you are going to participate in sexual activities, understand the ramifications. In addition to the possibility of contracting sexually transmitted diseases, you always run the risk of getting someone pregnant. It may be someone you want to spend the rest of your life with, a one night stand, or someone you were just kicking it with. Either way it goes, it’s not the child’s fault they were brought into the world, so step up to the plate and be in your child’s life. If baby momma is being petty, set up your child support and visitation directly with the courts. It's about the child, not the adults.

If you don't know by now, fathers matter. No matter what society tells you, a child who grows up without a good father figure grows up at a disadvantage. This disadvantage cannot be erased by attempting to substitute money for spending quality time with your child/children. Not surprisingly, having black father figures are the foremost differentiating factor in their child's quality of life.

Sadly, most black children never experience being in a two parent household. That's why choosing the right mate is important. In a study conducted by Pew, they found, "The living arrangements of black children stand in stark contrast to the other major racial and ethnic groups. The majority – 54 percent – are living with a single parent."

There are so many benefits for children who have two parents active in their lives. While I prefer that you are married, it doesn't always work out that way. Whether you are still with the mom or not, it is imperative that you remain in your child's life. Remember, the kids are innocent here and no matter how you feel about the mother, don't ever let that stop you from actively participating in your child's life. I know I keep repeating this, but the key word is "active."

You had the benefits of having your dad in the house with you. While I know that you didn't always see eye-to-eye, you know that he was actively involved in your life, athletically and academically. I wanted to point out the benefits of having a father (or positive father figure) who is active in your life:

- Children can only learn about being a male by having male role-models.
- Fathers often serve as the disciplinarian and are both more predictable and consistent with discipline.
- Fathers who are involved in their children's education tend to have children who perform better academically.
- Fathers spending time and giving focused attention can boost a child's sense of their own worth.
- Children tend to be more resilient and more confident when their fathers are actively involved in their lives.

- Fathers teach their sons how to treat women and they teach their daughters how to expect to be treated.
- Young boys learn how to be dads when they're older, and girls are more likely to choose a man who is likely to be a good dad to their children.
- Fathers who have a close relationship and set appropriate rules, can directly affect their child's ability to be persistent.
- Fathers foster that competitive spirit, especially for teenage boys to understand his position in the family and channel their strength in positive ways.

This list isn't all inclusive but demonstrates the power and importance of having fathers in children's lives. It's worth repeating, even if you and the mother of your children are not together, you owe it to your children to be active fathers in their lives. I don't care if she turns out to be the baby mama from hell, your obligation is to your children and not their mama. Likewise, if you get with someone else who doesn't want you to spend time with your children, LET HER GO!

Know this, there is only one perfect father and that's our heavenly Father! As fathers, nobody expects perfection, but rather active participation in your children's lives. Proverbs 4:1-6 says, "My children, listen when your father corrects you. Pay attention and learn good judgement, for I am giving you good guidance. Don't turn away from my instructions. For I, too, was once my father's son, tenderly loved as my mother's only child. My Father taught me, Take my words to heart. Follow my commands, and you will live. Get wisdom; develop good judgement. Don't forget my words or turn away from them. Don't turn your back on wisdom, for she will protect you" (NLT).

Love you to infinity and beyond,
Mom

Letter Eight Discussion

What were the key takeaways that you got from this letter?

____

____

____

____

____

____

____

What are your views of your father? Was he active in your life?

____

____

____

____

____

____

____

If your father was active in your life, how has that shaped you into the man you are today?

____

____

____

____

____

____

____

If your father was not active in your life, how has that impacted you?

____

____

____

____

____

____

____

Why do you believe that fathers are important in a child's life?

____
____
____
____
____
____
____

If you are currently a father, are you actively involved in your child's life?

____
____
____
____
____
____
____

What steps do you need to take if you know being a father is not in your plans right now?

____

____

____

____

____

____

____

Letter Nine

Friendships

9

"A friend is there to help, in any situation, and relatives are born to share our troubles."

Proverbs 17:17 CEV

To my talented young kings,

When you were younger and started school, I used to worry about you making friends. However, it was always amazing to me that by the end of the first day of school, you declared that you'd met your very best friend in the world. Each year this happened, sometimes the friends from previous years remained but eventually you always found new ones. When we moved multiple times and you didn't think that you would ever be able to find friends like the ones you left, you did.

As you have gotten older, your circle of friends has gotten smaller. Some may think that is a bad thing, but true friends are hard to come by. If you have a small circle of friends that is even better. Proverbs 18:24 (NLT) says, "There are "friends" who destroy each other, but a real friend sticks closer than a brother."

Let's examine this word friend. According to the Cambridge Dictionary, a friend is "a person who you know well and who you like a lot, but who is usually not a member of your family. This brings to mind the late 1990's song by Whodini called Friends (go find it and listen to it on Youtube). The very first verse says:

It's a word we use everyday
Most the time we use it in the wrong way
Now you can look the word up, again and again
But the dictionary doesn't know the meaning of friends
And if you ask me, you know, I couldn't be much help
Because a friend's somebody you judge for yourself.

As you get older, you do become more selective of who you allow into your personal circle. And if you haven't started evaluating those in your inner circle, please do!

Growing up, I used to hear that people come into your life for a reason, a season, or a lifetime. And that's how it is with friends. There are some friends who come into your life for a specific reason, maybe to help you adjust to a new school, a new job, etc. Think about when we moved, you had friends to help you adjust both times; some you kept in contact with and others you didn't. This doesn't minimize your friendship, the friendship just ran its course. There are some friends who come into your life for a season…football season, basketball season, AAU, youth church, high school, college, etc. Once the season was over, some of the friendships didn't last beyond that season. Again, this doesn't minimize the friendship, just another demonstration that the friendship ran its course. The last type of friendship, lifetime friendships are those special ties with people who have been with you through a reason and even a season and they are still around.

You see, those friends all play a vital part in shaping you into who you are today. But with that last type of friendship, lifetime friends are the ones you need to make sure you keep around. Those friends sometimes even seem more like family than friends. Lifetime friends can be counted on to tell you when you are doing something stupid, the same advice you didn't want to hear from your parents! Those friends tell you the truth even if it hurts. Those friends want you to succeed because you succeeding means they succeed.

If you find yourself with a 'friend' who kicks you when you down, who won't tell you that you doing something stupid, who only wants to talk about themselves, who never has time to listen to you, who talks about you when you are trying to do right, get rid of them right away. Some friends are toxic, they drain your energy and they can't help it. Get rid of them. The old folks used to say, misery loves company! Minimize your time with miserable friends.

And yes, I've had miserable friends who I just had to minimize my interactions with. I also have a few friends who will tell me when I'm doing something stupid, have on too much makeup, tell me when my wig is crooked, or tell me not to wear that outfit again! But they are also the ones who encourage me when I'm down, pray with me and for me, laugh with me, and are some of my biggest cheerleaders! I thank God for them every day.

There is a lot of research that talks about the importance of friendships to your emotional well-being, your maturation, your ability to get jobs, and the ability to gain new friends. Proverbs 27:17 (CEV) states, "Just as iron sharpens iron, friends sharpen the minds of each other."

So you should know where I'm going by now... There will be times where even the best of friends will let you down; but, don't worry because I know of someone who sticks closer than a brother, and that's Jesus Christ. When you're feeling all alone, you can talk to Him and He won't judge. Just pour out your heart to Him and He will be there for you. He will put the right people in your path to help you.

I will leave you with this, John 15:12-15 (MSG) sums it up perfectly,

"This is my command: Love one another the way I loved you. This is the very best way to love. Put your life o the lines for your friends. You are my friends when you do the things I command you. I'm no longer calling you servants because servants don't understand what their master is thinking and planning. No, I've named you friends because I've let you in on everything I've heard from the Father."

Love you to infinity and beyond,
Mom

Letter Nine Discussion

What were the key takeaways that you got from this letter?

____

____

____

____

____

____

____

How many 'real' friends would you say you have?

____

____

____

____

____

____

____

In your opinion, what makes a true friend?

____

Do you consider yourself a good friend? Why?

Do you have people in your life that profess to be your friend, but deep down you know they are not really down for you? What should you do?

____

____

____

____

____

____

____

What steps do you need to take to rid yourself from ?

____

____

____

____

____

____

____

Letter Ten
Forgiveness

"Instead, be kind and merciful, and forgive others, just as God forgave you because of Christ."

Ephesians 4:32 KJV

To my talented young kings,

Why a letter on forgiveness? Because the act of forgiveness is more critical to you than you can imagine. When I talk about forgiveness, I'm talking about the act of consciously deciding to release feelings of anger, hurt, resentment, or hate towards someone who has done you wrong. In Ephesians 4:32 (KJV) says, "And be ye kind one to another, tenderhearted, forgiving one another, even as God for Christ's sake hath forgiven you."

Please hear me loud and clear, the act of forgiveness is for YOU and not for those who have done you wrong. Also, forgiveness is not forgetting what happened, it's consciously choosing to forgive the actions of those who wronged you. It's not about giving someone a free pass, it's about freeing yourself from those feelings of anger, hurt, resentment, and hate. Most importantly, how can you expect God to forgive you for your sins, when you won't forgive others. Luke 6:37 (CEV) says, "Jesus said: Don't judge others, and God won't judge you. Don't be hard on others, and God won't be hard on you. Forgive others, and God will forgive you."

We all, even me, have done things that we are not so proud of. Maybe it's not telling the truth, disobeying your parents, cursing, drinking, sex, or any other bad habits. What you hold onto is how the enemy comes in and uses it against you. Remember I talked about daily affirmations, this is why forgiveness is so important. If you are so busy remembering all the things that you have done wrong, how can you ever step into your purpose?

So you have made some questionable decisions, the key is to forgive yourself. You can't change what happened but you can change your future response. Ask yourself these questions: Who are you now? Are you the same person who is still making questionable decisions? Do you have a new vision for yourself? Who do you want to be? God is quick and just to forgive our sins once we repent, but we hold onto the guilt which doesn't make a lot of sense.

How do you begin this path of forgiveness? You have to start by forgiving yourself and that paves the way for you to be able to forgive others. I know, I know, this seems easier said than done. If you follow these steps, it will become easier for you.

Step #1: Pay attention to your thoughts, your actions, reactions, behaviors, and moods. Leave your past hurts where they belong, in the past.

Step #2: Ask yourself, "Who upsets me the most?" Listen to the answer. Don't overthink it. (I know who that person is in my life.) Next, ask "Why does he/she upset me?" Once again, listen for an answer. Then ask, "Is this really true?" Listen for the answer.

Step #3: This step is probably the hardest to do, because it's going to force you to dive deep into the root of the problem. You may find that you have placed unrealistic expectations on yourself and those you have allowed into your life.

Ask yourself: What expectations do I have of the people in my life? Are they being fulfilled? If you answered yes, then great! If you answered no, you need to ask yourself "What are they not fulfilling?"

Then do the same thing for yourself: What expectations do you have for yourself? Are you meeting your own expectations? If so, great! If not, you need to ask yourself, "Why am I not meeting my self-expectations?"

Step #4: Forgive yourself and those in your life who didn't meet your expectations. Adapt and/or change your expec-tations.

I know you are saying, I hear you but… So, just think about this, Nelson Mandela served 27 years in a South African prison. He later wrote, "As I walked out the door toward the gate that would lead to my freedom, I knew if I didn't leave my bitterness and hatred behind, I'd still be in prison."

If we are honest with ourselves we will find that our anger, our frustration, our annoyance comes from within. If you think about it, most times the problem is that we have expectations of anothers and when they don't meet our expectations, that is when we get hurt. Hurt people, hurt people!

Let me give you an example. You have a girlfriend and you are in a relationship, your expectation is that she won't be talking to any other guys since you are in a relationship, right? However, you happen to see her phone and you find her corresponding with a guy in her DM/PM/IM. You get mad, you're hurt, and you end the relationship. You then decide that you are not going to give another relationship a chance since the last one didn't work out. But if you practice the steps above, you would ask yourself if she knew your expectation? Did you all lay out clearly what being in a relationship meant? See how that works?

Have I ever had to forgive someone? Yes, plenty of times. But when I was younger, I could hold a grudge. In the end, it only hurt me, not the other person. The one person who I had the hardest time forgiving was my father. It took my mom several attempts for me to see why she was so insistent on me forgiving him (probably more than a dozen or so, see I'm not perfect). When I did, it was like a weight was lifted from me. What I learned was that I had certain expectations of him and because I never shared those with him, I couldn't hold him to accountable to those expectations.

In Matthew 18:21-22 (MSG), "At that point Peter got up the nerve to ask, "Master, how many times do I forgive a brother or sister who hurts me? Seven?" Jesus replied, "Seven! Hardly. Try seventy times seven." Do the math!

Let me leave you with this proverb by Alexander Pope, "To err is human; to forgive, divine. Forgiveness is the best revenge. It is very easy to take revenge but it is very difficult to forgive others. It needs a broad and great heart. Because of the material world we live in, it is common for a person to err but forgiveness is an attribute of God."

Love you to infinity and beyond,
Mom

Letter Ten Discussion

What were the key takeaways that you got from this letter?

If God has forgiven you, why is it often hard to forgive yourself?

Has someone you cared about hurt you?

How do you deal with being hurt?

Have you hurt someone? How would you want them to approach you? Why would you expect them to forgive you?

____

____

____

____

____

____

____

Forgiveness is more for you than the other person. Do you believe that? Why or why not?

____

____

____

____

____

____

____

Letter Eleven

Fear Not

Be strong and of a good courage, fear not, nor be afraid of them: for the Lord thy God, he it is that doth go with thee; he will not fail thee, nor forsake thee."

Deuteronomy 31:6 KJV

To my talented young kings,

I know this title may seem strange to you, but you know with me there is always a lesson to be learned. Did you know that "fear not" is in the bible over 365 times? Yes, we are dealing with COVID-19, dealing with social injustice and dealing with everyday life, but if there are 365 mentions of it in the bible, you have a scripture you can read every day when the pressures of life get to you. Isaiah 41:10 (KJV) says, "Fear thou not; for I am with thee; be not dismayed; for I am they God: I will strengthen thee; yea, I will help thee; yea, I will uphold thee with the right hand of my righteousness."

If God is telling us not to fear, that means He doesn't want us spending our days being anxious or fearful. According to Pastor Rick Warren, "Because our hurts and hang-ups can often cause us to think that God is out to get us, that all He wants to do is condemn us and punish us. But that simply isn't true. Jesus is the proof of that."

No matter what society may think about you, no matter if you think you can't be the most famous, most athletic, most popular…you are the captain of your destiny. Never say or think negative things about yourself such as… I can never do anything right. I keep messing up. I'll never change. I'm dumb. Who could ever love me? Psalms 19:14 (KJV) says, "Let the words of my mouth and the meditation of my heart, be acceptable in thy sight, O Lord, my strength, and my redeemer." In other words, the way we talk and think about ourselves reveals how we feel about ourselves and directly impacts how we live our lives.

You need to speak good things about yourself in line with what the Word says about you. For example: "I am fearfully and wonderfully made in the likeness of the Almighty. He loves me so much he gave His only son to die for me. He loves me so much he knows how many hairs I have on my head. God created me and formed me with His own hands, and God doesn't make mistakes."

Start and end your day by declaring positive, biblical confessions. When you start to speak good, positive truths about yourself, you can succeed at being yourself, just the way God created you to be. So don't let anyone's negative perception of you cause you to doubt yourself. In the words of the late Congressman John Lewis, "Never let anyone - any person or any force - dampen, dim or diminish your light."

We all have fears but your faith has to outweigh your fear. That is the only way you can survive in this thing we call life. My job as your mom is to help you find your passion and your purpose, and do everything to make them a reality. But I can only do so much. You have to have faith in yourself and in your dreams. The late Nipsey Hussle even told you this, "You gotta go hard, you gotta believe in yourself. You gotta have a sense of humor to know that the bullshit is gonna happen. You can't be too serious about it or too emotional and fake when the bullshi*t happens. You gotta just stick to the script, believe and have an overwhelming confidence. Be your own biggest fan, your own biggest believer, and put it on your back and carry the weight."

The only person stopping you from fulfilling your dreams is you, it will never matter what anyone says against you or attempts to keep from you because what God has for you, is only for you. You have to stand up against the naysayers.

I have a lot of favorite poems, as you can tell. Marianne Williamson's poem, Our Deepest Fear (which is oftentimes credited to Nelson Mandela) sums up my feelings on why I push you to fulfill your purpose. She says,

Our deepest fear is not that we are inadequate.
Our deepest fear is that we are powerful beyond measure.
It is our light, not our darkness
That most frightens us.
We ask ourselves
Who am I to be brilliant, gorgeous, talented, fabulous?
Actually, who are you not to be?
You are a child of God.
You're playing small
Does not serve the world.
There's nothing enlightened about shrinking
So that other people won't feel insecure around you.
We are all meant to shine,
As children do.
We were born to make manifest
The glory of God that is within us.
It's not just in some of us;
It's in everyone.
And as we let our own light shine,
We unconsciously give other people permission to do the same.
As we're liberated from our own fear,
Our presence automatically liberates others.

I will end by asking you the same questions I asked in the first letter. What will it take for you to recognize that you are descendants of the most

High? A royal priesthood? That's what God's word says and I believe it. "God is not a man, that He should lie, nor a son of man, that He should repent. Has He said, and will He not do?" (Numbers 23:19).

Repeat this prayer as often as you need to. God, I'm done speaking negative things about myself. I declare the truth that You love me and accept me. I will be all that You created me to be.

Stop dimming your lights, my young kings, shine on into your destiny!

Love you to infinity and beyond,
Mom

Letter Eleven Discussion

What were the key takeaways that you got from this letter?

____

____

____

____

____

____

____

How do you see yourself?

____

____

____

____

____

____

____

What is your deepest fear?

____

____

____

____

____

____

____

Is your fear keeping you from living out your dream?

____

____

____

____

____

____

____

Is the fear of failing or the fear of succeeding keeping you from realizing your potential?

____

____

____

____

____

____

____

What steps do you take to get faith to outweigh your fear?

____

____

____

____

____

____

____

PLAY LIST

The songs listed below are some of my favorites. They represent all genres of music. If you get a chance, listen to the words of the songs. They tell of my love even when I'm not around to share them with you.

A Song for Mama by Boyz II Men
I Say a Little Prayer by Aretha Franklin
I'll Always Love My Mama by The Intruders
What a Wonderful World by Louis Armstrong
Unforgettable by Nat King Cole
95 Million Miles by Jason Mraz
I Hope You Dance by Lee Ann Womack
Dear Mama by 2Pac
The First Time Ever I Saw Your Face by Roberta Flack
Have I Told You Lately by Van Morrison
Mother's Love by Kem
Ain't No Mountain High Enough by Marvin Gay & Tammi Terrell
Have I Told You Lately by Rod Stewart
You Are the Sunshine of My Life by Stevie Wonder
A Song for You by Donny Hathaway
You Bring Me Joy by Anita Baker
If I Could by Regina Belle
We Are Family by Sister Sledge

Stand By Me by Ben E. King
That's What Mama's Do by Jason Matthews

READING LIST

When you get an opportunity, try reading one or all of the books listed below. There are hundreds out there and I probably just scratched the surface. These books and links remind you of your past, your current, and future.

The Mis-education of the Negro by Carter Godwin Woodson

The Autobiography of Malcom X by Malcolm X and Alex Haley

Roots by Alex Haley

I Am Not Your Negro Documentary by Raoul Peck (based on James Baldwin's Remember This House)

The Hate U Give by Angie Thomas

Just Mercy: A Story of Justice and Redemption by Bryan Stevenson

So You Want to Talk About Racy by Ijeoma Oluo

The Fire Next Time by James Baldwin

The Souls of Black Folk by W.E.B. Du Bois

Our Time is Now: Power, Purpose and the Fight for a Fair America

www.blacklivesmatter.com

www.facebook.com/fatherslivesmatter

www.naacp.org

www.nul.org

NOTES

Letter One

Carter, W. G. (1933) *The Mis-Education of the Negro*. Independently Published.

Baldwin, J. (1963) A Talk to Teachers. (Delivered October 16, 1963, as "The Negro Child - His Self Image"; originally published in The Saturday Review, December 21, 1963, reprinted in The Price of the Ticket, Collected Non-Fiction 1948-1985, Saint Martins 1985)

Letter Four

Warren, R. (2002) *The Purpose Driven Life*, New York: Zondervan.

Letter Five

freecreditreport.com

www.mymillennialguide.com/generational-wealth

Letter Seven

Shawn. (n.d.) *11 Things Real Men Do In Their Relationships By Shawn*, Retrieved from www.elcrema.com

Letter Eight

https://www.cdc.gov/nchs/data/nvsr/nvsr68/nvsr68_13-508.pdf

Reasons Why Children Need Dads (2014). Retrieved from www.parent4success.com

Black Dads Matter (2020). Retrieved from https://ifstudies.org/blog.

Letter Ten

Chopra, S., and Gina Vild. (2020). *How to Forgive Like Nelson Mandela.* Retrieved from www.psychologytoday.com

Pope, A. An Essay on Criticism, Part II, 1711

Letter Eleven

Weber, K. (2016). *Rick Warren: Why God Encourages Christians to 'Fear Not' 365 Times in the Bible*. Retrieved from www.christianpost.com

ABOUT THE AUTHOR

Dr. Mary L. Wise is a John Maxwell certified speaker, teacher, and coach. She offers workshops, seminars, keynote speaking, and coaching, aiding others in personal and professional growth through study and practical application of John's proven leadership methods. Working together, she moves individuals and/or teams or organizations in the desired direction to reach their goals.

Dr. Wise has spent the last 30 years serving in various leadership roles within the Human Resources industry. She has a Bachelor's degree in Business Administration from The University of Central Florida, an MBA from Embry-Riddle Aeronautical University, and a Doctorate in Organizational Leadership from the University of Phoenix. She has led, coached, and worked with teams, large and small, both virtual and in-person helping them overcome the challenges needed to become highly functional. She is a change agent who believes that we all must be personally accountable for our results. Her personal integrity and ability to get the job done is unquestionable and respected. One of her greatest strengths is her ability to connect with people at all levels within an organization.

Dr. Wise is the daughter of the late Tommie and Mary Lott. She is the wife of Antonio Wise, Sr.; the mother of Antonio, Jr, Austin, and Alexander and the Gigi of Zayden. She also is a niece, sister, and cousin to many. She also is member of Alpha Kappa Alpha Sorority, Inc (Alpha Tau Omega Chapter), and spends time volunteering with the youth at her church.

Dr. Wise is the owner and CEO of Wise Evolutions, LLC, which specializes in coaching, teaching and speaking for individual coaching clients or mid- to large size organizations. Her mission is to help you refresh, refine, and refocus. She possesses a strong passion to guide others to develop and enterprise solutions. She contributes creative energy and commitment to every opportunity she encounters as she has consistently demonstrated over her 30 plus years in the field of Human Resources.

If you are ready to push by your self-imposed limitations, ready to push further in your organization, ready to up your game or ready to lead your organization through the difficult race conversations, contact her at www.wiseevolutions.com. Additionally, she is also a certified DISC consultant and trainer. Here are the services she is able to provide to you and/or your organization.

Coaching
- Individual Coaching
- Group Coaching

Speaking
- Lunch n Learns
- Keynote Speaker
- Half day and full day workshops/seminars
- In-house corporate training
- Executive and corporate retreats

Teaching
- Leadership Gold
- Put Your Dream to the Test
- Becoming a Person of Influence
- 15 Invaluable Laws of Growth
- How to be a REAL Success
- Everyone Communicates Few Connect
- Leading Through Crisis

Contact Dr. Mary Wise at:

Wise Evolutions, LLC

10650 Culebra Rd. #483

San Antonio, TX 78251

Phone: 210.560.1263

www.wiseevolutions.com

wiseevolutions@wiseevolutions.com

www.ingramcontent.com/pod-product-compliance
Lightning Source LLC
Chambersburg PA
CBHW071130090426
42736CB00012B/2080
9780578779065